Endeavour

Chantelle Lowe

Endeavour

Anthology – Volume Three

Chantelle Lowe

All rights reserved. No part of this book may be reproduced or transmitted in any form or by any means, electronic or mechanical, including photocopying, recording, or by any information storage and retrieval system, without permission in writing from the publisher.

Published by Chantelle Griffin, originally known as Chantelle Lowe, in 2023

Interior layout by Chantelle Lowe

Cover by Chantelle Lowe

Photograph: Mount Wellington

Catalogue-in-Publication details available from the National Library of Australia

paperback ISBN: 978-0-6487786-8-4

Also available in hardback
ISBN: 978-0-6487786-9-1

Copyright © Chantelle Griffin, originally known as Chantelle Lowe, 2023

Dedication

In memory of my Aunt Dorothy, who would seek out the small side galleries, then with a loving patience absorb the subtle changes of every fine detail. Explaining the process behind each medium with care and admiration.

Contents

Endeavour

Achievement	1
A fraction in eternity	5
A little older	6
All and nothing	7
All I have endured	9
All is gone	12
All my might	14
An emblem	16
Annabel	19
Another time, another world	20
An inspiration (Rory Spence)	22
Art form	23

A space	26
Away from disappointment	27
Be in peace	28
Beyond borders	29
Black	30
Blame	33
Blue	34
Breathing	36
Broaden my horizon	37
Bushfire	38
By choice	40
Cascading down	41
Cautious destiny	42
Cities and deserts	43
Clarity	45
Cold air	46
Cold sky	47
Colour of sadness	49
Come the rain	50
Complexity	51
Controller of destiny	52
Core	55
Courage	56
Cradle Mountain (Dove Lake)	58

Creating reality	65
Culmination of fear	66
Darkness around	67
Deceit	69
Deceiver	70
Delicate	72
Delusion	73
Depths of the river	74
Depths of water	76
Destroyer	79
Did anyone know?	82
Dilemma	83
Dirt	84
Discomfort	86
Distant memory	88
Domeney's Fruit Farm	89
Dragon calling	90
Dragons fly	93
Dream	94
Dreams unread	97
Drink to the death of lies	98
Dying day	101
Elsewhere	102
Embers of infinity	104

Embrace strength	106
Entity	107
Evolution	108
Exiled dragon	109
Existence	110
Fear sets in	113
Feel at home	114
Feeling of home	115
Fight	116
Finding time	117
Fire	118
Flames	121
Foe	122
Footprints	125
For all that I have risen for	126
Forest deep	129
Forgotten dragon	132
Formation	133
Forward	134
Freezing	135
Future bold	136
Glassy depths	137
Greater cause	139
Great hope	140

Green	142
Hold my own	143
Hollow	145
Hope beckons	146
I have far to roam	149
Insignificant	152
Inspirational space	153
Intolerant	154
Isolated	155
It eludes me	156
Julia Gillard	158
Just me	159
Know not where	160
Lay to rest	162
Leave this world	165
Light	166
Lost from sight	168
Memories I had	170
Misled	171
Moment to decide	172
Move	173
Moving shadows	174
Much to be	175
Murder	176

My best	177
My opponents	178
My world	181
Near sea	182
No end	183
Of consequence	184
Of gratitude	186
One miss	187
Open sea	188
Opportunity	189
Other spaces	190
Overturn	191
Passing storm	192
Pathway to eternity	193
Peaceful dragon	194
Peace in the dawn	195
Pieces that stand	196
Precipice	197
Purple	198
Reality	199
Realm link	200
Real toll	201
Red	202
Relax	203

Resistance	204
Retrospect	206
Rise and soar	207
Rivalry	208
River running	209
Rivulets	210
Say it soon	212
Search of relief	215
Shall fall	216
Shimmering secret	219
Silence followed	220
Soft black	222
Soft blue	223
Soft green	224
Soft purple	225
Soft red	226
Soft wind	227
Soft yellow	229
Solitary being	230
Still searching	232
Strength	233
Strength in voices	234
Substance	235
Table of time	236

Tactics	237
Take me away	238
Take no ones hand	241
Take the past away	242
Taking grasp	243
Talking	244
Taunting	245
The chase	247
The forgotten land	248
The humble architect	249
The intrepid walk to eternity	250
The sea of reason	253
The sea turns	254
The soldier of dusk	255
The timid	257
The way it had to be	258
Thinking about Burnie	260
Through the gloom	263
Time eternal	264
Time to unwind	265
To be confident	267
To be strong	268
To crush myself	270
To end the pain	272

To flee	275
To know who I am	276
Traces left behind	278
Transgression	281
Trembling	282
Turmoil	283
Undetermined path	284
Ultimate goal	285
Vanish	287
Virus	288
Waiting for friends	289
Washed away	290
Was it important?	291
Waves folding	292
Way ahead	293
What could be	294
What holds me	295
What I have become	296
When my path was for one	297
When no one calls	299
When the wind blows	302
When rain turns to thunder	304
Within a place	305
World apart	307

Would it matter? 308
Yellow 310

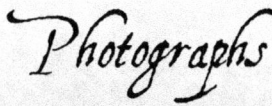

Photographs of Mount Wellington, 6 March 2022

4	100	228
8	112	240
18	120	246
32	124	252
44	128	256
48	138	262
54	144	266
64	148	274
68	164	280
78	180	286
92	214	298
96	218	306

Acknowledgements

I would like to thank Greg Lowe and Sally Shaw for their encouragement.

Forevvard

Every gasp rang through with a hollow edge, seizing in a shallow pit of emptiness within the vacuum. Deepening the ever approaching struggle as an unenviable rattle clung to the last of each exhaled breath. Weakness set in, clambering through the steady stream of rushing air as it held at bay the crashing tide.

Yet in the darkness there remained hope, as the lady leaned in, 'Don't let anyone tell you that you have to stop.'

Chantelle Lowe

Achievement

Here I am,
not knowing what to do,
and I hope I have the power,
of a lifetime of thought in my hand.
My breath is taken away,
from me,
with the great feeling surrounding,
my consciousness.
I wonder if anybody else,
can feel as I do?
But I know that at this point,
no one can.
This is someone,
who had no future and no past,
who only lived for the present.
For the present,
was too horrible to look upon.

Chantelle Lowe

Now I have my goal,
now I have found that inner peace,
so long ago lost.
I feel ashamed,
that I do not think others wanted,
me to have this.
But I have found it,
it makes me sad,
when I should be happy.
This should be one of my most happiest,
days,
but so many have wanted to tell me
that
I
would never reach it.
I know I have proven them wrong,
I do not want them to see my
happiness.
They will destroy what I have,
what I have given my life for.
When they thought they could give
my life,
for themselves,
to something else.

Chantelle Lowe

I know at this time I am free,
but what I have dedicated myself to,
far outweighs,
those who have hated me.
I have achieved,
this on my own.
This is my greatest power,
my power of
achievement.

Chantelle Lowe

A fraction in eternity

A sentence in a word of time,
a fraction in eternity.
A drop amidst a stormy flood,
a shadow on the darkest night.
As a glimmer catches the daylight hours,
it is time to go home and sleep.

Chantelle Lowe

A little older

There is time in which we find ourselves,
not knowing which way to go,
all the while time passes,
and I grow a little older.

All and nothing

Time can create harmony,
but in this case it is obscene.
Nothing can create harmony,
where there was none.
For here I am all,
and for you there is nothing.
Creation made it that way,
who am I to argue,
when there is nothing left for you.
I can see my future lying ahead,
it comes to take me away.

All I have endured

Eclipsing the time that pressed upon the land,
a way ahead through the ever setting rain.
For the paths diverge in the place where I stand,
not knowing if the hoard will be loss or gain.

There are many times when I have wondered why,
the harsh caress of turmoil does take plight,
across the trails that web through sea and sky,
to reside at arm's length, in plain sight.

For I have not known many days,
that weigh a memory kinder still,
where love and laughter ruled the ways,
of a life I carry on to fulfil.

No stranger moments that have arisen,
from the timely reminders that lay fresh,

Chantelle Lowe

in the turmoil of an unseen prison,
where coldness, warmth and feelings mesh.

A true epiphany takes hold in hand,
of an outstretched path laid bare.
A way ahead to greet the final demand,
in the lock of old time's snare.

Colours dance across the early sun,
as the creep of morning wakes.
An eternal race when all is done,
and the unknown path it takes.

For I have seen many come and go,
with the ease of the passing tide.
Slipping away into the fading flow,
as all will eventually abide.

The turmoil creeps with a steady gait,
of futures it does unduly bind,
on a mindful resting fate,
careless of the figures it will bind.

A time for turmoil from within the soul,

does reckon with the gaps of joy,
searing through old memories whole,
plaguing the actions that do deploy.

For peace is a road rarely travelled,
though highly sought in dismay,
a culmination of thought unravelled,
through presumptions showing the way.

No greater moment was tried and sought,
than the call that time begot,
of a loving hand through turmoil wrought,
bringing with it an ease long forgot.

A memory of a peaceful grace,
holding tight the warmth of day,
keeping an even steady pace,
in its own kind and unassuming way.

All is gone

Does the world revolve, around a single thought?
When day has come, and must go,
back into the night.
Is all lost, when no one sees the coming of the dawn,
and no one hears the presence felt?
Is all thrown away,
with one last say?
Screaming, eternally born.
Is this the way that all must die,
when no one hears the final sigh?
I hear no remorse, to what is done,
when found left standing, there is none.
I hear the heart ache and beat,
left standing by the vacant street.
When all is lost,
all is gone,
all is quiet,

Chantelle Lowe

all is done.
No death awaits me now,
in this place of oblivion.
I wake and wonder, to what disgrace,
who would have dared make such a place?
But yet I find no answer comes,
for truth be told, could anyone
not see, that this is our disgrace?

All my might

In the night I saw him flee,
to pursue what was inner most set.
How could I not have seen,
what lay before the rest.
This time I knew for sure,
what had been and gone before.
Now that all had been undone,
for the lost, and now unseen.
To fight the only hand,
which could have caught the night.
Yet I knew there was no one,
who could see the dying right,
of what was left alone,
until the final sight.
I had no presence here,
where once was all my might.
Though now they knew,

Chantelle Lowe

with all certainty.
Desired for none,
was what I sought,
though knew I never had.

An emblem

No one can see the emblem of the structural balance,
which holds so swiftly against respite.
To me, I see no other flaw,
which could perpetuate such redemption.
Will I ever live to see the peace,
in eternal night,
only broken by this insanity,
by which is lived in light?
Do I not see the lies foretold,
streaming from the spark of life?
In which no darkness swells,
to take away the pain.
For I see not,
the hope of immortal black.
For, writhing in frustration and agony,
I see only insanity,
curling forth onto the sharpest knife.

Chantelle Lowe

But this, this life,
is not to see the ray of light,
which burns away all flight.
All hope of ever reaching what is right,
within my little grasp.
For I have seen,
the peace of all creation,
which has lived in place,
of all existence.
Though I know it for what it truly is,
the spell of eternal life.

Annabel

Perhaps one day we will meet again,
when the wind is fleeting past.
A tiny shadow remembered then,
as the sun's rays hold and last.

Perhaps we will meet in a spring breeze,
without any troubles or woes.
A fleeting spirit carried with ease,
as far as the rainbow goes.

Perhaps when I am old and grey,
I will hold you in the morning light.
We will cheer and play,
as the sun beams down so bright.

Then I will feel your tiny presence,
filled with such warmth and effervescence.

Another time, another world

I feel as though I have been there before,
this is all old to me and I cannot see a way out.
But this is not the end,
for me at least for I shall live on,
in another time,
in another world,
I will always be there.
Forever hiding, seeking, destroying,
so that life itself will live on.
In my hand,
holds new races, new problems, new solutions, new risks,
this world is not ready for,
until it has destroyed itself.
As in all remnants of its past will have deteriorated
then the world will expire in preparation of the new one.
One hopes that this new race shall behold more intelligence than us,
but then,

Chantelle Lowe

look around at what we have accomplished,
and for every step forward,
environmentally and psychologically,
we go backward.

An inspiration (Rory Spence)

A glimpse of imagination in a pool of time,
swirling thoughts and raising hopes.
An imagination which runs so deep it envelopes eternity,
and I see it, glimpsing reality, a master of creation.
An autonomy of a piece in time,
inspiration, and I hear it call forth.
It seeps through the waters of time creating eminent ripples,
carrying with it the future, and what is.
A placement in time, a key to the door of knowledge,
enveloping the fragile world and all its ideas.
A path into other thoughts, questioning, always thinking.
Intrepid is the soul that I find caressing the earth in all its grace,
and yet it has more humility than most people can lay claim.

Art form

Most people are time gatherers, wanderers, etcetera,
searching through a phase, travelling back and forth.
Changing anything from little pieces of information,
to something more traumatic,
something that would change everything in its path.
It's not a wise decision, some are rather foolish,
but if you turned everything upside-down,
and started all over again.
You may find something of use,
something to help you understand,
this immense little piece of transformation,
into something, more well known, more elaborate,
and especially more intriguing.

But not many know the art,
though many may say they do.
This art is specifically rare,

especially when you are hunting down,
its purest form.
I say this to you,
because it is well and truly known,
you have found its beginning.
Ah, but reaching the end,
that is truly another matter entirely.
Some may never reach the end,
some may not want it,
some like myself may try,
to achieve the end,
though perfect has its hazards.
I am not trying to discourage
you in anyway.
On the contrary,
I am merely explaining that no matter,
how well you try,
there will always be a new level,
for you to strive towards.
You will always be able to improve,
and you will always be able,
to become even more talented,
in your art.

Chantelle Lowe

You may wonder what is this art,
it is an inner flame,
the core,
eternally glowing within you.
You cannot dowse it,
though you can make it stronger,
and brighter.

That is the art,
and I hope that in one of your kind,
the spark has many more years,
in which to flourish.

Chantelle Lowe

A space

Time,
for all eternity.
Place,
which is meant to be.
Rising forth,
spilling over,
taking place.
In recollection,
of a space.

Away from disappointment

This is the place I see,
this is everything,
into the darkness I go.
Out into the cold and unknown,
where I have not been.
Placing a hand on my shoulder,
keeping me safe.
Keeping my head up,
away from disappointment,
and into the skies above.

Be in peace

In harmony we shall conspire,
upon to see,
and when the darkness turns to fade,
we shall call again.
And in the image of the warmth,
I shall be in peace.

Beyond borders

There is one light that shines beyond all others,
and it dares to dream beyond all doubts,
beyond the borders that block the mind.
Yet all we see and all we hope for were not enough,
is it so much to dream, when dreaming is not enough?
Walk out the entrance to eternity, the path that leads to empathy,
it escapes me, what I will find.
I want to find hope, I want to find everything,
yet that is not what it is meant for.
Please forgive me, please forgive me,
for what I have done is not enough.
It was far too much to stay within the dream,
as the waters lapped in, and I drowned in the idea.
Does this have to be? When reaching out is so difficult.

Black

Black hides by herself in caverns of time long forgotten,
to call upon the souls deemed to live in the past,
and blanket the earth with her comforting essence.
When you fade away with time she will store the knowledge you had,
she is a condensation of all emotions without expression,
with the experience of infinite without the finite to come.
She wraps herself in coarse cloth of the darkest possible night,
it has tattered edges that match the frayed wisps of her hair,
which hang loose from the fastly tied bun pulled back from her fine features.
She is a nomad, a conqueror, a deceiver, but never a betrayer.
A very well known intellectual, with no cunning or basic plot,
she passes to the direction that time makes for her, but never interferes with it.
Her mind is always blank though she is more than capable of thinking.
She is the watcher of all that happens, the judge that time has given itself,
her ideas are made and carried out by others.

Chantelle Lowe

Yet her personal self steps everywhere with small fine shoes so as not to leave an imprint,
so greets the soul of black.

Blame

Truth read, truth unsaid,
blame unknown, blame not mine.
Created in the most evil depths,
not meant for me,
though I was there, and easy prey.
It picked me out, its cowardly form.
Evil not meant for me,
it picked me out,
I was there.
Evil and cruel intent,
hatred running so deep,
from a person who should have known better.

Blue

Blue trudges through the dew ridden pebbles, making a lulling grating sound,
newly worn boots which keep out the wet, sodden earth.
Neat, common, heavy clothes to pass by the wind when it tries to gallop through,
a braid holding back the shoulder-length crop of thick hair.
Experienced eyes watching out of familiar markings,
hand on hilt for something to hold onto.
A decisive and hesitating mind though always prepared,
walking with an uneven yet almost constant pace,
strong and flexible muscles used to being worked.
A very proud individual,
exerting effort to attempt anything she thinks she is capable of doing.
She is not afraid to hold her head and state her profound view,
though she prefers keeping her thoughts to herself.
By looking at people she can read who and what they are,
she chooses her every word carefully so as not to cause unnecessary

Chantelle Lowe

trouble.
A contemplater at every turn though never stopping too long,
she is the invisible past seeping through to the present situation,
a knower of decision.
So concludes the form of blue.

Breathing

Standing tall in the midst of gloom sweeping down with disarray,
I know not where it came in brightness of day unfolding in the sun.
A tremor in the prevailing breeze shifting with it the hopeful sway,
yet not long would it tamper with a glimmer finely left undone.

Call upon it as to a small and fearful child playing in the sand of time,
a glimpse of reckoning in the ambient hour reaching on to eternity.
Sadness struck deep within from a source known hidden in the grime,
yet every calling brought with it knowledge still shining with ability.

No force was struck upon this day as it folded in the dimming light,
a memory of searing pain filtered at the edges dulling in the gloom.
A pace of the intensity in the mind as it wrapped around the night,
for no struggle came without the sound of the distant calling doom.

As it will in the raging seam that followed down the line of sight,
while taking hold the caress would falter giving way under all my might.

Broaden my horizon

To broaden my horizon,
to widen my path,
to excluding the dark ending,
that lay on my path.
To take hold of my past,
to look deep in the future,
to see with wide eyes,
what is my present adventure.

Bushfire

I hear it cry within the night,
calling to pry out the patient.
With silence deep it gathers form,
while all do sleep in cold night air.
None hear the call across the sky,
until the toll is seen nearby.
I hear it come up closer still,
as only some have time to see.
I whimper in my heart so cold,
though flames fly thin, the heat does scorch,
and all I see have run in hope,
as there is me to catch them up.
Now flames are tall when all make haste,
and heated wall comes closer still.
I run into the cold night air,
seeking a new path to follow.
Those I have lost I cannot find,

Chantelle Lowe

to hear the cost I see behind.
High flames draw near in spiralled heat,
the calls I hear chill my own heart.
In soul I hide but not in truth,
fire rolls like tide as wind seeps through.

By choice

The mutual feeling of accomplishing something,
a deep, deep surging from within.
Old and forthcoming from the deep,
intuition in its way,
it plays on my toes,
and tingles on my spine.
Here I have come from so far,
against all the wash of the tide.
Something that never would have been,
had things stayed as they were.
I am grateful for knowing there is more,
than the life I had before.
A life not mine by choice,
a life hidden and concealed.
I took my life,
and I made it,
out of the ashes of the old.

Cascading down

Pressure cascading down the slope of a warm winter's day,
it transfuses itself at a point near the sea.
Call forward the many colours and shades of grey,
for this focal point is what we have come to see.

It laps us in with its open arm,
shaping characters long gone to the past.
An island of sanctuary in a bubble of calm,
an envelope of time folds away in shadows cast.

Seeping through are the images around,
placing identity on this small space inside.
For here is the place where community is found,
facing a sea of people and the rising tide.

Inspiration flows deep into the thoughts of those who peer,
on the possibilities that have arisen here.

Cautious destiny

As the wanderer fell into the dimness,
it looked up to see the grey sky.
The moon called, with its peeping shadows,
it walked on towards destiny,
and peace.
Not so on the path it had travelled,
no rest, the moon the first light,
to set eyes upon its cold grace.
For a long time it stared,
wondering,
but now, not now and not here.
It saw into the dim light ahead,
nothing had pressured it, but it came,
standing, then cautiously moving,
forward,
into the dim peace.

Cities and deserts

Waving the fan of a delicate chill with the tip of a finger,
freezing still the monotonous moving in their world as they stand.
Praying the density of turmoil won't let the thing linger,
in the obsolete reign of misfortune amongst the towers and sand.

Fumbling wildly through papers belonging to the forgotten land,
where the people screech of their madness, stirring in misery and pain.
Somewhere beyond I can feel them calling, reaching out their hand,
to me alone, in this unworthy place I wish I could refrain.

I see in the shadow of your fingers the distillation of fear,
that shall I seek to come above all else to overwhelm me.
And will also comfort me in my own fragmented mind of despair,
lays with it the courage others lack all together and which I see.

Clarity

All is as it was, and inside I filled with the greatness,
knowing this is what it was to me.
Memories gathered from my past,
seeing me as I was, and what was there around me.
In this I was, that was the way it had to be.
Only a glimmer of knowing, a small insight into something
catastrophic.
Yet I know beyond all clarity, that this is what it was.
Hoping, knowing, I did yet I did not.
This played in my world and here I come to stand.
A place which calls to me, a name I know.
It calls to me and I know it.
It hears me and I know it,
it was me.

Chantelle Lowe

Cold air

Tonight is cold I see,
and the air is sharp.
The damp air I breathe,
slowly turns my nose to red.

Cold sky

Sea, sea,
come smother me.
Take me in,
come let me see.
Tide, tide,
come smother me.
In ice cold sky,
there I shall be.

Colour of sadness

Empathy, sympathy, what do you care?
When I hear what goes on,
then I prefer to know.
Knowing is everything it could be and more.
To meet you on equal terms,
then know, that I am stronger.
You are left in a past impression,
sweeping your illusion of the world.
Then I am here in reality.
A cold harsh reign,
seeping through all my veins.
Colour of sadness,
creeping up on me,
calling it by name.

Chantelle Lowe

Come the rain

Come, come the rain
and its glorious thunder.
Pulverising the ground on which we stand,
to defy our structure.

Chantelle Lowe

Complexity

In the term of uncertainty,
the inevitable happens,
in a recurring structure.
To implicate the other form,
in the gratifying task,
of ambition.
In coupling the serenity,
of the complex issue,
in time will for hold.

Controller of destiny

Shrivelling the environment.
Complaining of sin where there is none,
taking over what there is to control,
am I here, there, or everywhere?
When this ends what will I be,
the controller of destiny,
perhaps?
Complain to me over in the corner
if you must,
complain a little harder.
What was it you said,
I didn't really want to hear.
Calling me when I am not there
will do no good.
Lie, and lie again,
and wonder why I prefer the truth.
Perhaps you knew?

Chantelle Lowe

Then you always did.
I wanted you, then I didn't know much.
Knowledge can leave
an endearing legacy.
It can place me here without you.

Core

What is this form which seeps,
through my mind and fears.
Creating little pathways,
connecting to a core.
A plan which settles unresolved,
in the area of the area in space.

Courage

There are places in my heart,
left torn wide apart.
My recollections are dim,
of the life I lived in.

It is difficult to find,
the path through my mind.
One I have not seen yet,
one which lies unset.

It wavers, so fragile,
when I hold it for a while.
Let it have life and grow,
and deepen the all mighty flow.

Into the space which covers the dark,
and let it brighten and spark.

Chantelle Lowe

May it deepen into the courage,
that swells across my rage.

Cradle Mountain (Dove Lake)

In the dancing reflection of the deep lake.

I saw time's eye leap up at me,
from the blackness of despair,
the lake it appealed to me,
the depths of knowledge it held there.

Underneath its layer the mystery,
of the days as they fled past,
and up there in the hills I saw,
no clouds or their shadows cast.

Still was this day I saw to me,
broken only by the helicopter,
but what a sight to see,
as the track was taking over.

Chantelle Lowe

The rangers were busily painting,
we watched from the car while waiting.

Lake Dove was no Mount field,
with the tumbling water fall.
No trace of large great boulders,
making entire hillside walls.

But it left a trace that lake,
deep in my feathered mind,
a lake so black and deep,
the bed floor would be hard to find.

The water's edge rippled past the stones,
lapping at my feet on the shore,
the boat shed showed the signs,
of harsher weather from before.

The shoreline with its unusual shapes,
carved out from the water's edge,
making little lookouts,
for people standing on its ledge.

I crossed this path looking back,

to the group of busy faces,
trying to catch a little rest,
before heading to other places.

In my eyes was the Cradle Mountain,
for which I had no recognition,
this journey was a surprise to me,
not knowing the destination.

A few minutes I did share,
after a long hard walk up hill,
with the surrounding, glancing 'round,
not wanting to stand still.

All I heard of this beautiful place,
was 'beware, it's dangerous',
the snow can fall on a sunny day,
and turn to harsh from glamorous.

My only glimpse was sunny and fine,
I didn't know quite what to say,
but as I waited for the others,
I knew it was unusual in its way.

Chantelle Lowe

This journey which I came along,
left me with a dream,
of something small and wonderful,
an idea which made me beam.

I knew the moment was small and fragile,
taking form in scribbles on my page,
listening to the presenter,
and his voice of experience and age.

I knew as soon as it was done,
my formal drawings did not compare,
to an idea pure in form,
drawn with loving care.

I knew the form, it was transition,
from one place to the other,
transporting the occupant,
from one world to another.

I took it in my hand this thought,
freeing my mind and soul,
glimpsing the picture in my head,
of the finished product, whole.

Chantelle Lowe

It took me away to another time,
in the page of memory's mind,
a glimpse of childhood somewhere else,
in the stories left behind.

A young flame of curiosity,
which led me to explore,
away from the shabby old huts,
past imagination's door.

I fled down the old animal tracks,
leaving safety far away.
Here there are many duck tracks,
for humans there to stay.

I wandered a little near the water's edge,
as if I were a child,
bringing back playful curiosity,
on that day, warm and mild.

No maps of paths,
did I hold in my hand,
a hesitation crossed my face,

Chantelle Lowe

as I took a moment to stand.

I searched my eye across the lake,
looking up to the crystal sky,
reality had taken the myth,
as I looked up and said goodbye.

Chantelle Lowe

Creating reality

This is the world I live in,
not to mention everything else,
which crashes in around.
Appose and we shall see,
what it is that you wanted to be.
Taking hold of the small luck
which circles the earth.
Creating an alternate picture for one's self.
creating reality.

Culmination of fear

Killing is eternal,
in the essence of time.
It culminates the fear
of many,
and feeds on the darkness
of the soul.

Darkness around

The turmoil runs deep into suspicion, creasing the brow of the aged,
coming down from the darkness that fell over the edges.
A darkness that closed ever tightly around
the hands and fingers of the weak,
drifting over the sky and shadowing the thoughts of many.
Into this darkness stepped the resolute,
determined and unwavering.
A silhouetted figure reaching forward never failing
as it breaks through the cold dull howls.
A figure strong and unyielding, never giving way,
to the darkness that surrounds.

Deceit

These are days of treacherous times,
filled with the calmness of deceit.
Overlapping the soul of importance,
creating demise and defeat.

Deceiver

Hold my hand,
and spin with the tide.
For I am mightier,
than the force that spins your future,
into a web of deception,
and lies.
For I am the truth,
all mighty and powerful,
I burn through your soul,
and find your deepest secrets.
To hold them up to the sky,
and show what you are worth.
For I am cold,
and crystal clear.
I am the shock,
which shatters hope,
and creates new beginnings.

Chantelle Lowe

But am I what you seek,
in your darkest hour?
When the rain calls for your blood,
and I am there to take it.

Delicate

I see the colours fading into the wall,
as I approach the centre of the floor,
the ceiling is high, amply double height,
and the paintings hanging are so delicate.

Delusion

Oh, is it your way to delight?
In witnessing my suffering,
with not a care of anything,
banishing me away from sight.

What was it that you hoped to gain?
In deluding me all the way,
to see what purpose I might lay,
then leave my lone self to remain.

When did you have the final word?
To end it with no peaceful ride,
and kill the dying hope inside,
to leave the soul truly battered.

Depths of the river

The cold extends its shiver,
as the ground is gone from my feet,
I left my world behind,
filled with a calm and stagnant heat.
My limbs so fresh they walk,
upon the enveloping cold,
the resources of my warmth,
flow out to meet the current hold.

I have nowhere to go,
my body sinks,
gaining the weight of outside pressures.
My voice is hollow,
my blurred vision looks back at the shore,
I can make out a figure.
Then my head ducks,
and my arms are pulled by the massive current,

Chantelle Lowe

like the weight of my inner turmoil,
I am pulled down.
By chance my head breaks the surface,
and the figure still stands,
but my strength is gone,
and my thoughts are strangled.
I can slowly feel my legs sway,
then they are gone,
the river is like a warm blanket,
it covers me,
then I am gone.

Chantelle Lowe

Depths of water

My weight is pulled under,
dangerously low,
yet I can manage,
I have no trouble here.
My books that hold my world,
lay back at the shore.
I am calm and distant here,
as the cold splashes over my soul.
I feel the bottom,
I cannot get up,
I move and move,
slowly catching a glimpse
of the perpetual light,
balancing through my eyes.
A solitary figure stands,
glimpsing only my head,
then gone,

Chantelle Lowe

the current takes my full weight,
as I harness it.
But I am gone,
as my head weighs down,
in desperation I pull up,
but the force fathoms resistance,
and my head sinks.

Destroyer

Why is it so strange,
that I feel a loss.
Someone I had forgotten,
very dear to me,
that broke my dreams.
I had nothing,
not hope, not pride.
Why should I feel pity,
when it was not me,
who broke a silent prayer,
to be happy.
It was not my fault, what I did,
I broke free,
of eternal madness,
of eternal suffering.
Why do I have to die,
for someone else's name,

Chantelle Lowe

when they should die for their own?
To take me with them,
would be the greatest sin.
But I did not go,
I did not die,
I would not have killed my soul for someone else.
To live, and be dead,
be nothing,
is a tragedy beyond relief,
I wish I did not suffer,
but I do,
at someone else's hand.
I want to break free,
but inside I cannot.
I left,
I kept my soul,
but damage had already been done.
Every day I grow,
grow away,
grow out to who I am,
and when I look back,
I see pity.
Pity because I see a person,
who tried to destroy who I am,

Chantelle Lowe

and instead of caring,
broke my soul,
and instead of mending,
broke it further.
I cannot show pity,
for a person of hatred and anger,
with no guilt.
No guilt for actions which hurt,
beyond memory,
beyond pain,
I have no pity for that person.
I have no pity for the person,
who wanted to destroy my soul,
and in turn destroy my life.

Chantelle Lowe

Did anyone know?

Spirit find me calling home,
giving me a hand.
But in all extremity,
did anyone know.
I wish I could have told,
but no one helped.
Instead I find myself,
wondering why.
When things could have been different.

Dilemma

Come,
come as you are to the place where
I am.
Who am I,
when you are not the one to judge
me?
The creation of my soul,
was fused with the eminent
integral parts which take place in time.
Can I discern what is not?
When what is not is here,
and I am faced with the dilemma
of confusion,
because I am no longer where I was.

Dirt

Death to all who appose
the great and mighty deed,
the steady permanent downfall
which caresses the very edges
of my soul.
I am the source,
which feeds the mist
that rolls steadily over my body,
but I am calm,
and delicate.
The mover of time,
with every crumbling I create.
I am a destroyer,
a self supported host.
I perpetrate many
with the lust of greed,
of what may be hidden

in my cover.
Yet I am also a taker,
replenishing myself with your flesh.
I know you are there,
I feel your every footstep,
your every motive.
Gravity compels me
but I am also corrosive
and destructive.
Yet you are perturbed
on turning me to your whim,
but I am my own,
as is seen.

Chantelle Lowe

Discomfort

The air shimmers with every stride,
through disparage and dissolution.
Which covers the walls eternally,
and seeps down the long unhealing drapes.
This room which I have made for myself,
covers my soul in a warm filled blanket.
Remembering is the hardest thing,
but forgetting would be even harder.
To see myself like this,
and know that I have grown beyond.
To a play which leaves me strong,
to face those that kept me at bay.
But to my discomfort,
I come back to myself,
and with everything,
I know I have come farther.
Through the hall of healing,

Chantelle Lowe

and into the world beyond.

Distant memory

Encumbering time, in the most facetious way.
Traditionally tragic, though not very caring.
Dipping into the untimely fray,
gripping the bottom of reality,
as though it were the only hope,
not wanting to know why.
But then inside, I feel it go,
a distant memory clinging on,
and I find myself asking why.
In a place where cold reaches out,
and inside I have a little doubt,
but not much against the blue grey sky.

Chantelle Lowe

Domeney's Fruit Farm

Rustling through leaves on a hot summer's day,
a dull dry air carried along with no breeze,
taking the breaths of the workers away,
collecting under the iron shed so as to tease.

Smoke gathering across the crystal blue sky,
dulling the reflection of the water below,
here a second home holds itself high,
replacing the 'Cerisy House' burnt long ago.

Green leaves slowly replacing dark cherries,
a mass of activity all around to be seen,
making the graceful old couple feel at ease,
covering boxes with cherries in between.

Rustling through leaves on a hot summer's day,
one by one all the workers go their way.

Dragon calling

When the cold wind blows,
and I am inside,
the scenery turns to dust,
but I am here you say,
then walk outside,
and see what lay ahead.
For the cold wind blows,
with the coming of dawn,
and the old grey edge of dusk,
but where have they come from,
where did they go,
when the night falls steadily down?
In the cold wind blows,
the cries of many fallen,
taken in to heal the cuts,
for when we all come back again,
it shall be there waiting,

Chantelle Lowe

for the one who has fallen last.
Now the cold wind blows,
where no one travels,
though we all hear its cry so husk,
when time draws near,
and it must go,
will all who embrace it follow?
And the cold wind blows,
so deep and hollow,
though all must know it is thus,
and in the end,
when we peer 'round the bend,
its call is sharp and tense.

Chantelle Lowe

Dragons fly

In my room I see the dragons fly, comforting me with their sadness,
I am not alone here, they are here,
it is peaceful and quiet, in my little room.
I am here, I am here, but they do not hear,
though that does not matter, when I leave.
For I will always be able to come back,
to leave again,
but it will always be there,
for in myself it dies alone and quiet,
waiting for me to follow.

Dream

They never knew me,
as I reached out my mind.
I couldn't see,
I couldn't see.
But I hoped,
beyond all eternity.
Come closer,
come closer.
And I did,
as the last ashes
of life blew out.
The cold seeped in,
I felt it hold,
but it wasn't
me it took,
off into the distance.
I fell with it,

Chantelle Lowe

but it didn't grasp me.
As I lifted my head,
I knew,
it had gone.

Chantelle Lowe

Dreams unread

There is one light that shines beyond all others,
it shines so bright I cannot see the path ahead.
As the breeze sweeps through and smothers,
it takes away my dreams left unread.

Drink to the death of lies

She,
the one betrayer.
Cold and silent,
with her delicate hand.
I crossed it once,
so long ago.
In mine was the hand of death,
the hand I gave,
the death of lies.
She,
the enchantress,
the true witch.
To her my hand did serve,
until she used my life,
as precious blood upon her gown.
My blood was poison,
against her skin,

Chantelle Lowe

for truth is the sharpest knife.
She,
the vain and elegant,
with painted smile.
I offered her my cup to drink,
the death of lies,
which fell from her mouth.
For 'tis death I give,
in hand and blood,
drink to the death of lies.

Dying day

This is not the time,
to see beyond the distance.
To see what has been before,
even when all has returned to the undying hand.
With all which has been lost,
to all the undying thoughts,
which roam unheard,
to this dying day.

Elsewhere

In lavender dreams I rise above,
not knowing the circumstances
which can flood through the system.
Whichever way this apathy continues
it is likely to overcome the revenue of naturalism.
Creating discourse throughout the century
beginning a new whole in which to divulge.
As I see it this is creating antipathy
which in verse creates autonomy
but which, if either, sits first?
Am I to reconcile to a baby,
with little intelligence, or its mother?
Whatever the case it should be said
that this is not the predicament
which faces me now, at this very moment.
For on these steps of time,
as I see it, though not very clear,

Chantelle Lowe

it should be that all of us is,
when we are not what we are.
Truly this colour should shed light
on the matter, although it might not be the case.
In which the path should lead elsewhere,
anywhere, but not here, or so it seams.

Chantelle Lowe

Embers of infinity

I took a little dip once,
in the pond of life,
stretching out beyond me,
a dark and fearsome tide.
The embers of infinity,
reaching up inside.
I was a little stronger,
a little looser, deep inside.
A rhythmic tow pulled me under,
taking me for a ride.
To places I'd never been,
mimicking the abstract guide.
All in a little hollow lay,
the questions sprouting out.
All the while my mind wonders,
opening the door of doubt.
Something in me yearned and burned,

Chantelle Lowe

to rage and shout.
After all the things that had been,
and the past which I thought about.
A hole wedged into my mind,
left there from people gone.
Mimicking serenity,
in their tiny minds for so long.
All this time I learn,
that alone, I have to be strong.

Embrace strength

Sage of winter,
palm of north,
meld together
and bring me forth.

Strengthen my success,
and my agility.
Prepare my soul,
for what is to be.

Breathe life into my veins,
caress my being.
Taking hold of weakness,
in the final ending.

Embrace strength.

Entity

Life, the eternal word.
Everlasting, ever changing.
Ever seeing over the whole,
not knowing which way to go.
Playing in a world stripped of entity,
a world without a care.

Chantelle Lowe

Evolution

Time is evolution of the soul,
passing through eternity,
giving way to nothing.

Chantelle Lowe

Exiled dragon

In the west,
the eastward dragon lives,
for all to see,
and hear.
He is,
the hidden creature.
exiled from day,
to give its life to mist and shadow,
hating to be found.
It hides away from any creature,
in hope never to be found.

Existence

Come,
strip my soul of all desires.
Take as you have left,
with no grain of intuition.
This substance you walk,
holds no mercy,
for those who call it foe.
To reach, yet not be deceived,
by those who surround and undermine,
is not to be truthful,
but to relinquish all unseen harm.
This is the recognition,
of pittance beyond grief and sanity.
A time to mislead,
yet conquer,
is too extravagant,
for the unseen.

Chantelle Lowe

Time is still to unfold,
virtue by any means,
but to control,
and dominate beyond belief,
is seldom otherwise.
But to see,
with all feeling,
and know not what,
when all is clear,
is to see the undying.
Where existence,
is not where I exist.

Chantelle Lowe

Fear sets in

Disappointment as everything falls down,
the turmoil of the end slows steadily,
not knowing which way to go.
All the while it sees nothing,
as the dim dark light fades,
oblivion takes over and pummels us forward.
At this point the fear sets in,
it takes over the outer fringes of the body,
making a stronghold yet unseen.

Chantelle Lowe

Feel at home

The object and feeling of being home,
having a sense of belonging.
Having fun and laughing,
being with friends and smiling.
A place where I can be me,
and everything is all right.
Where I can be creative,
and I can move ahead.
A place where I can truly feel at home.

Feeling of home

You know who you are when you look around.
This is the place you knew a world away, yet here it is.
Bringing you forth into a new dimension.
A place which is more than what it can be.
Seeking out strangers and old friends,
calling itself home in a welcoming landscape.
This old friend, only recently built,
singing tales of old times,
old ways,
old lives.
The place where you stand,
you look around,
you imagine.
You think of what it was, and what it has become.
This little island, where people used to come and go.
A place where you can stop and chat, and meet friends,
and somehow it feels home.

Fight

A fight,
against a future so wrong,
against all the odds.
Defiance of cruelty,
defiance of neglect.
A fight,
for a life worth having,
for respect.
Against everything that has happened.

Finding time

No time has come,
for me to part.
Where from this place,
I have to dart.
What knowing is,
the last disgrace.
And finding time,
is the eternal race.

Fire

A page of mockery is all I see,
withered to the bone.
I've come a long way here to be,
as passers hear my tone.
I am a catalyst you see,
with an all and mighty groan.
But here I can be seen as small,
if someone does take care.
Although the matter is for all,
the moment I say 'dare'.
Then everyone resounds the call,
through hot and withered air.
My time is one you all will know,
with a crash and whirling spin,
but I am the pressure with one blow,
the striking from within.
But no one hears my coloured show,

Chantelle Lowe

unless they are close in.
It matters not the outside view,
as I topple in and sear,
for here all things look different too,
in the lock of old time's sneer.

Flames

Oh hear the multitude of pleas come prancing,
through withered wind with ease as all go by.
Life stretches out its arms to those,
as gathering in calm in centre flame,
as screams wither by in cold pursuit,
though not all hear it pin its victims thus.

Joe

I heard your voice,
deep and fatal,
but I was not here for you,
I stood alone,
and strong.
The wind bled through my skin,
and I felt its sorrow,
as harshly as I saw your face,
so close to mine.
But I was not alone,
in my beliefs,
they were iron against your cold flesh,
shattering the ice,
for all to see.
This was my hope,
this was my glory,
to all who had been betrayed,

Chantelle Lowe

including myself.

Chantelle Lowe

Footprints

Wash away the hopes and fears,
that flow onto the shore.
Leave behind the warmth and tears,
that did not show before.

Coming through the water's edge,
sparkling in the sun;
broken shells with secret knowledge,
of footsteps made by one.

In between lies silk soft sand,
cushioning every blow.
As small feet leave trails on the land,
towards the water's calming flow.

Here, this person stands but brief,
to find a short and calm relief.

Chantelle Lowe

For all that I have risen for

I feel as though,
tomorrow I will go,
through fields of everlasting
reign.
Where devastation is thus
on my brain.
To conquer all seven
seas,
would be as hard as the reject
of my pleas,
and I would gain less
from it.

Though I skim the floods
of my break,
The tides may turn
let for my sake.

Chantelle Lowe

Come forth to be,
as one I rise,
To sear my mind,
for compromise.
So deliver me hence,
to steady my sense,
For all that I
have risen for.

Forest deep

The rolling of moss and fern,
the old growth of the forest deep,
this is something I have come to yearn,
in the city where shadows creep.

I have tracked over mountains of rock,
great boulders with gaps between,
I gave others quite a shock,
as I merrily jumped over the scene.

The smell of the moist air fills my breath,
letting my imagination run wild,
with seas of travellers gone to death,
trekking through this ancient field.

The river runs trickling waterfalls,
miniature sprays of shining sun,

Chantelle Lowe

it melts any stresses down the walls,
created by trees in line as one.

Occasionally small doors are made,
by rock hidden in the earth bed,
and trees fallen around to aide,
meandering paths for others to tread.

The ferns near the rushing water,
smell of mist and old decay,
renewing the forest later,
as the cycle goes its way.

I tread along the little trails,
and I see the sky so clear,
my astonishment never fails,
as my journey does appear.

The sounds of the small bird calls,
and possums make their rounds,
beside my small tent poles,
scavenging in places out of bounds.

The night sky brings the wallaby,

Chantelle Lowe

its movements small and timid,
it looks around in the clumped debris,
of the tents where it once hid.

Damp air smothers my skin,
stirring old memories, deep from within.

Chantelle Lowe

Forgotten dragon

In the darkness of the faith
let the dragon come to soar over eternity,
for all to see.
The power of its voice shall be heard,
echoing the time lost and forgotten in the shadows.

Chantelle Lowe

Formation

If I wanted I could see over the rolling hills,
not wanting to look, rolling one's eye over the landscape.
Writhing, wriggling, changing, causing motion,
causing thought, creating thinking.
Thinking turns the wheel, turns the words,
makes transition, makes formation.
Breathing, bleeding, sweating over the task at hand.
Ammunition for the soul, recuperation,
manifesting itself;
a statement.

Chantelle Lowe

Forward

Creation is the assembly
of the image,
coherent in the visual
mind.
Place it on the sea,
and demolish it to the ground.
What have you achieved,
in this space of nothing?
Am I the only eminent
soul,
which sees straight forward?

Freezing

Water on my tips so cold,
what future is it that you hold?
When face of mine does show all clear,
when eyes of mine in depths do peer.

Cold lashes out on arm of strength,
when body travels its full length.
As wind perpetual friend or foe,
wakes up and freezes head to toe.

Future bold

I see the new sight, loud and clear,
from what a lonely life, I lived and breathed.
I could not go back to see the fear,
from desolation I had received.
For now I know all crime has gone,
whence left in destruction.
All who knew the kind to be strong,
stronger than that of cause and admission.
I know I left what had been lost,
through the unruly gain of sacrifice,
to someone else's hand, my cost.
For now I know the real life, which does entice,
me from what was never mine, to hold.
Though now I see the future clear, through eyes of bold.

Glassy depths

The ecliptic soul finds its home on the shore,
the space existing for such a short distance,
the perimeter in the landscape.
A small and fragile line drawn around the lake,
penetrated occasionally by people's feet.
So smooth is the sunlight gleaming off the stones,
shining brightly white in the warm afternoon sun.
The sky reflects the clarity allowing the light a steady stream,
warming the skin and the soul inside.
Short is the time, a memory solid,
stepping out into the foreign flora blanketing the earth,
swirling into the glassy depths,
of the lulling black lake below.

Greater cause

Screaming past the palette of time,
it tempts me to see,
the origin of the sacrifice.
The overwhelming desire,
to give into a greater cause.

Great hope

Where are we headed, in this world of doom and gloom?
Where the lights are all hollow,
and shading the past.
This world of shrivelled hope,
in the realms of the unknown.
Into this fear I plunge,
with my ever burdening soul,
keeping me on my feet,
and consuming me whole.
Now I know the world
is a very dark place,
with things left to conquer,
and new challenges to face.
This is where I bring myself
farther ahead than I have been.
To break out of the old world thought,
and take on what is unseen.

Chantelle Lowe

Striving to achieve the ultimate gain,
where others have come to travel.
Taking with me great hope,
and seeing what may unravel.

Green

Green is a pagan soldier, walking through the dust,
bruised and swollen feet, inside hard an aggravating boots.
Sunset behind her back, streaming her shadow long and dark,
cool winds swooping up from the south, playing with her cloak.
Soft clear eyes peering down, touching everything with a small gaze,
hesitating to consume the detail, of a widely gathered place.
Free at last from the taverns of hate, its fire faded,
left with a peace of resounding, throughout the distance.
The people had brought an optimistic hope and it had devoured everything,
even the anger of ignorance.
Now everything had its rightful path, even the soldier of green.

Hold my own

Perhaps the tides have turned,
for what you say?
Perhaps I am no longer there,
with all that had been ripped away.

No hand to hold me tight,
in a direction of unseen horror.
Why do I prefer the peaceful night,
to this unseen terror?

To hear the calling, not so far,
of a life better shown.
Where I can see you are,
and I will hold my own.

Chantelle Lowe

Hollow

Somebody saw me,
through the ice and snow,
with nowhere to go.
I was dangerous, and vexed,
cunning through respite.
Though no one knew my face so dark,
hollow to the edge,
I was the killer queen.
The ice cold stone,
which lay hard against my face.
Like the time of feeling,
which reached me through agony and pain.
To see the light dawn anew,
on misery and insanity so extreme,
and yet not see the darkness of silent peace,
through the harsh evil of dawn.

Hope beckons

I hide in the glimmer of time raging far beneath the crystal sky,
a glimmer of hope beckons me on the driest day and dreariest night.
A calling forth of time and energy beckoning like an eternal sigh,
the dreams of many caught in an infinite web hurled into the light.

For I reach the thoughts of many glimpsing into the unforeseen,
but is it the reasoned hand that takes away so many dreams?
In a glimmer of turmoil and a force to be reckoned with so mean,
yet time will call it and fetch it forth into the rushing streams.

A caller that time forgot so rare opens up the revelling tide,
taking forth the strongest hold among the ever reaching to aspire.
For all that will become and see no more in the like that will abide,
a simmering glow of rectitude holding into a place filled higher.

But no hand will reach for the light is dim fading in wanton haste,
covering the indistinguishable flame as it taunts from a distance.

Chantelle Lowe

Taken to the dust in the ever dying hold by the will of the chaste,
it beckoned once with an intimate grace holding a final stance.

No more will the skies cry or the rivers bleed knowing a murky fear,
as the broken grow strong and the humble in the time that will appear.

I have far to roam

No matter how far the road is, that I travel,
I always seem to find, in vain,
the string of time, as it unravels,
but not the hope that will remain.

To see the life that once was led,
as I know it to be wrong.
In darkness did I feel the tread,
of the hand which held me strong.

Now I see the clear blue skies,
raging, all forlorn.
And I feel myself rise,
to the knowledge I was free-born.

I see myself again,
on that all and mighty plain.

Chantelle Lowe

It is hard to remember then,
in the emptiness that remains.

Now I do not see the living cold,
which, in my days brought so much fear.
And now I know the truth foretold,
from all the hate that did appear.

As I look back in time I know,
what was done, was put to rest.
With one final flight, to undergo,
that last and horrifying test.

But still I know within my heart,
the secrets I have churned.
They plague me now, when I am apart,
of a life that lived and burned.

I breathe my silence from a faded time,
and look upon the future rare.
As all that I have risen is mine,
in this lonely palm, for which I care.

I see the long and outstretched path,

Chantelle Lowe

which has been waiting for me.
It makes me smile and want to laugh,
to know where I will always be.

I see the fading time gone by,
I reach out, I am not alone.
I see my hand reach for the sky,
for here, I have far to roam.

Insignificant

The light crosses the shadows in
many different ways.
Covering the little whispers of the past,
tracing every insignificant move.
Taking away from the unforeseen.

Inspirational space

Aspiration and celebration of space,
to be made, as to be seen.
With all the definition of place,
in the way that things have been.

I have come from a time as any other,
to drive the force of perpetual being.
When reminiscing is not enough to gather,
those to the place of seeing.

Where everything has been taken apart,
in the misguided information,
and I am there in the centre heart,
giving to the strong foundation.

Where places are made with the hands of old
paving the way for the art to unfold.

Intolerant

Time in the world is only for one,
creating a path this way and that.
Looking forward and looking back,
what is it that we have done,
to make this world seem so intolerant?

Isolated

Why can't I be free,
in a world so desolate,
and filled with debris,
is this my chosen fate?
To stay in a world of chaos,
where there is no hope in sight,
and there is a great sense of loss,
in the place that was so bright.
Am I ever going to find my way out?
When everything is against my dreams,
and all I can do is shout,
while others tear at my seams.
In this world so desolated,
will I become so isolated?

It eludes me

There are times when I wonder what I am doing,
whether this is enough?
There are times when I wonder what my decisions
will lead to?
Because all the while I see my decisions unfold,
I am not sure what they mean.
I am not sure why I am doing this,
why I am searching in this way?
There is something that I have overlooked,
yet I am not sure what.
Is this the way I should be doing things,
when it seems to lead to nought?
I feel as though I have trapped myself,
deeper into an unknown position,
not knowing where it will lead.
What have I been missing to do that?
What am I overlooking?

Chantelle Lowe

It seems as though the answer could be so close,
yet it still eludes me.
I am forever running around in an intertwining loop,
which does not seem to want to unravel,
and it leaves me wondering where I am.

Julia Gillard

When the day is said and the gloom is swept away with the sun's light,
there let it be known a lady as no other that stood like none before her.
A shoulder held high in the grasp of the all mighty task taking plight,
and in this moment held tight the visions passing forward to confer.

A winnowing breeze calling the masses at ease as she strode to the stand,
for this time of restitution would hold within reason and thought.
Wiping the dreams into ambitions flowing out into a world so grand,
with it came compromise with the burdened task and a resolution sought.

A heavy platform weighing with every step taken in a firm held grace,
for no one had stood upon the prominent path with such vindication.
A leader with the willingness and strength to hold every goal into place,
rising in a dutiful elegance to the challenges of the leadership position.

With grace and dignity shone a star so bright above the raging turmoil,
a perfect accomplishment left behind in the legacy of her greatest toil.

Just me

Time is not the way or the reason.
It is just me,
fleeting with opportunity,
taking a chance above the rest,
being the optimist,
when there is nothing to be optimistic about.

Know not where

When you take this page,
when you see what you see,
then you will learn,
that not all is as it seems.
A destroyer of the carrier of faith,
glides into existence,
from the deepest day of despair.
Here I am,
here I stand,
I know not where.
Take me as I am,
for I am no other.
Inside I know who I am,
do you?
All this nonsense takes hold,
and I find it hard to see reality.
I am alone,

Chantelle Lowe

being who I am,
no one will walk this path for me.
This is what makes me
an individual.

Lay to rest

The creation of the mind took over hatred,
but where would we be without lies.
I wanted to know if something could be changed,
I found my answer, but it was not what I wanted.
So I took what I found and I accepted it.
I let all my tormenting lay to rest,
I gave that person away, the one which did not accept me.
I knew it was the right thing to do, one of the hardest things to do.
I gave away that which I was supposed to accept.
I gave it away because it did not want me,
and in some ways I knew I had not wanted it.
Something which society expected me to have,
I gave it away, I discarded it as it had once discarded me.
I had to be without it, as I knew it was for the best.
I took it upon myself to become what I was,
and become it I did.
The all and inspiring person which fate had made me,

Chantelle Lowe

yet I would not achieve until I stood alone.

Chantelle Lowe

Leave this world

Calling,
away and it calls me,
wanting me to go.
Wanting me to leave this world.

Chantelle Lowe

Light

Do you think that it would be,
without me?
I am the one and all,
the perpetrator,
the under taker.
But am I real,
as all the others?
Are yes,
and much, much more.
To look at my face,
would be a crime,
but there are many faces,
you see of me.
Is this one real,
or that?
I am the whole,
the essence between your feet.

Chantelle Lowe

The step that makes
the whole world move forward,
I am that, and more.
To deny me,
would take oblivion,
but do you have that long to wait?
I ask you many questions,
and I give you many answers,
but are they the ones you want,
or is it more?
The great unknown,
to see me out,
but I am a traveller of time,
a destroyer,
a defeater,
and a killer.

Chantelle Lowe

Lost from sight

Do I hear your voice so true,
in the deadening of all who strive?
To be as one you knew,
when all fled
far from all you had ever touched.
Did I see the single hand,
with all its might?
Lay down upon the land,
those who fight.
Was it worth that last river of blood,
which tainted so many souls,
and washed away the worth of hope?
Did I hear your voice so true?
When everybody else who knew,
had gone and left you too.
Then why, with all your might,
did you raise your sword to fight,

when all was gone and lost from sight,
and I was left with none?
For what had been done,
on that fateful night,
shook the whole,
and held it tight.
Did you not see, that I saw too,
the misery that had been cast on you?
From all the dispassion,
you held in your heart,
to come to difference,
that we must part.
But how I left,
you never knew,
why it had to be.
As you could not undo,
what you had done,
to me.

Memories I had

Come into the light,
come out from the cold.
What is it that I remember to be,
when all has grown old.
It plagues me at times,
all the memories I had.

Misled

To be misled,
repelled, betrayed.
To be relinquished from sin,
untold in name and glory.
To be free from prejudice,
and the most senile mockery.
To play the game of cards,
and not win,
yet not be beaten.
To survive the harshest climate,
which can never be wrought.
To destroy hope,
in all reason and name,
is to be controversial,
to the most mortal question,
which lingers in denial,
and sears all minds.

Moment to decide

As I was pondering there and then,
I reached upon a motivating decision.
It wasn't rather big, well actually rather small,
and just seemed to creep in, while I was getting rather bored.
I don't know why it said hello,
just there and then it began to go.
It was really immense I think,
well beautiful anyway.
I rather enjoyed its company while it lasted,
upon this fine day.

Move

To describe the innocence of the time,
it is difficult to discuss.
When shattered dreams created hazards,
of which were made in hate.
It is clear to me,
that none of this was meant to be,
though it happened all the same.
It is what should never have been,
this I cannot explain.
Though I live with memories from this time,
I move onto further ground.

Chantelle Lowe

Moving shadows

Black is the colour of her hair as she moves,
the colour of the cloak draped around her shoulders.
It covers her small dainty shoes,
and the chain around her neck.
She moves graciously through the shadows,
whispering out names.

Much to be

Today, no place calls home,
I see the wandering grass,
raging through the earth,
and I know this,
is the desert of my dreams.
I want to fall away,
where no one else has been,
and share in a way I can see,
where one has not yet seen.
I know the day gone longer yet,
in travel and dismay.
To see on the road what lies ahead,
to show the unknown way.
Yet I see, in all by night,
the eternal raging light,
and I know there is much to be,
where no one has yet to see.

Murder

Though I kill, I kill by night,
to stab in my pool of glee,
thy enemies shall never see,
towards the forbidden light.

I find, a need to open,
their weak, thinner hearts of woe,
shall be split upon their show,
to distinguish their bad omen.

I crave and devour their flesh,
to still and maintain my rise,
of my dim shadowy size,
as on which their souls I mesh.

There around I state my pledge,
there aground I lay my ledge.

Chantelle Lowe

My best

To the whole which has been and gone,
to the mighty which have lain to rest.
To all who have not known which is real,
do I know that I have done my best?

My opponents

Despairingly, I must forgive my opponents,
their airs and graces that make my life difficult.
The essence of nature aligns them to another fold,
and here I am walking an increasingly different path.
One step ahead, while three steps behind the others,
that have the advantage of time and their peers.
I am left to wander a lonely path,
not quite in one field and not quite in another.
Playing between the two,
not quite knowing which will seek me out.
One tall and proud,
the other spread out and secretive.
Both strange and intelligent in their own separate ways,
calling out to me, making expectations of me.
Neither docile or placid to the touch,
keeping rhythm and playing their own game.
Not much can be said except that both are strong,

Chantelle Lowe

unbreakable and foreboding when up close.

Chantelle Lowe

My world

Eclipsed by eternity, taken over by poverty.
Entrapped in turmoil, burdened by pain.
Collapsing down into irrationality.
Burning into absence of the soul,
for this is where I leave.
And escape to a whole new reality.

Near sea

By my side lies,
the open wind,
with its majestic arm.
It surrounds me, for metres,
nothing but sun can penetrate it,
and the cold sea air.

Here I am,
and here I be,
back at my own place,
by the sea.

No end

Who shall stop the young,
when they have been carried away?
Who shall stay behind,
when there is nothing left here?
Who will suffice for the beginning,
when there is no end
for all eternity?

Of consequence

Chronicle of the past in depth,
placing the time; unfold.
Which way do we go from here?
When light turns into dark,
and out of darkness
comes the truth.
Truth decides
the price of consequence.
When consequence means so
little.
Chance to move and
change the world
in ways before,
and ways not gone.
Chance to take hold
of what remains aloof.
To the realm of consequence

Chantelle Lowe

which deceives us all
into dysfunction,
which creates the chaos
in which we live.

Of gratitude

Time to collect aspiration and configuration.
an intrepid soul reaching out.
Reaching for something collectively massive.
An intuition rising forward.
Burdening the intrepid figures rising forth.
An abolition taking form,
out of the darkness rising forward.
Creating ripples on the ocean,
a little murmur of recognition,
of gratitude,
exhaling in the moment.
Enjoyment from knowledge,
from finding that which is interesting,
and reaching for it.

One miss

Pain,
suffering.
I feel my body crumble,
in the heat.
I can't find my way,
I'm dead on my feet.
No river,
no plain,
no contours the same.
Can I trip?
One miss, and fall.
Raging torrent deep inside,
thought sinks at the peril.

Chantelle Lowe

Open sea

I command thee ocean be calm, be still,
settle and rest till our trip is done.
Give us safety on our travel,
from the end to the time we have begun.
Protect us in your mighty arms,
while we are on the open sea.
Take us back safely,
to where we ought to be.

Opportunity

Analysing the compensation,
being ready to show the find,
coming forth with information,
not caring if you mind.

Tapping on the window,
an opportunity left aside,
showing how far I will go,
to uncover what you will hide.

I know the opportunity is slim,
I will give it all I have got,
even when things look grim,
and you think that I forgot.

The avalanche you did so well,
will not be anything upon my spell.

Other spaces

Placement of the unseen,
coming forth through uncertainty.
Taking away the lives of many,
producing animation.
Taking hold in others thoughts,
where other spaces used to be.
Instead this is left,
untouched and unkept,
in a very unruly way.
Taking up the minds of others,
plaguing contemplation.
Breaking through to the unseen name.

Overturn

Open the door and you will see,
open the door to imagination.
I felt a drip on my hands and it fell,
it caressed my soul, the path of intuition.
Oblivion criss-crossed my path, but I could not see it,
the framework of desire, hope and longing.
Fortune stretched its form laying out before me,
I drew it near, into the clutches of seeing.
How desperate was I to overturn,
the lucrative monolith reeling forward.
It seeps over, covering the dreams of the creative,
holding onto the final word.

Passing storm

Weathering the brunt of the storm,
as it passes over.
The figure at its centre stands isolated,
pictured in the most eternal way.
Marked by the seeds of time,
growing through the ages,
covering the soul over with its frayed edges.
Capturing the energy from within.
A tumultuous time rushing ahead,
laying out a treacherous and unfulfilled path.
It takes the soul along in its tidal arms,
slowly pushing behind the figure,
supporting its stride,
making the way forward.

Chantelle Lowe

Pathway to eternity

The pathway to eternity,
the pathway to see.
A greater step forward into this world,
a presence felt.

Peaceful dragon

In the winter comes,
the deafening roar,
of the dragon,
sweet and soft.
But loud,
and intense.
The sound of calmness.

Seeps quickly,
through the land.

In every heart
it finds,
Will bring,
health,
and everlasting
peace.

Chantelle Lowe

Peace in the dawn

As the waves crashed down on the shoreline,
I knew that in my hands I held peace.
As truly as the dawn came, it was mine,
fragile as the sun's rays which did not cease.

Pieces that stand

Place it on a leaf and float it down the river,
 give it a place in time to wear away.
Come back and see the things that quiver,
 into the background and fading day.

Place the shadow of what was into the plan,
to see the significance of the pieces that stand.
 To allow to weather, distort and tan,
 into the lost, not forgotten in hand.

With this the knowledge that came before,
which was now gone, down to the written past.
 To enrich and create upon even more,
 as a passage of time has come to last.

Even though the new is reborn on the old,
some gather to make their souls known; sold.

Precipice

This is my moment, I stand on the precipice of time,
looking down upon all that I have done,
for now I can stand alone,
leaving my past behind me,
yet grasping it in both hands.
Taking it with me in pride and grace,
for in this world I do not have long.
I hold my hand up high to reach the stars,
as I once did wishing with one now gone, on a small dream.
I hold out all my fears for others here to see,
and the grief I have known as the future I do not fear.
Yet in darkness I will strive,
with shame and hurt now gone.
There is but one thing I have left undone in this world,
and now I let it fly up to the stars to reign free.

Purple

Purple rules supreme, it gives the final say on everything,
how we live, how we die, where we go, what we do.
She has the power to wield everything for herself,
to do as she so desires, free from any higher power.
She holds her head high and moves swiftly,
nothing escapes her knowing, wisdom is her.
Moving with an ease of gracefulness,
keeping her plots a mystery from the ever watchful eyes.
Well groomed, tied back hair, expressionless lips,
a forth-right stare, neatly presented formal garments.
In her own environment, with the recognition she aimed for,
so seats herself the intuition of purple.

Reality

A desecration to reality.
An eminent source,
which was the reality at the time.
I took it back.
I did not need to, but it was something I did.
Reaching back from the afterthought.
Reaching back and knowing.
Knowing all, and yet wondering forever.

Chantelle Lowe

Realm link

As I hear my name I call,
I hear the future pass.
As I hear the real toll,
of the present and the past.
Seek out those I find,
together as we stand.
With our spirits for which we bind,
is not the everlasting whole.

Chantelle Lowe

Real toll

Together, no life is just,
to each, one other may trust.
No life in a hand,
no word in the sand,
of the path yet ahead,
where no one has read.
The word which binds a goal,
to what is the real toll.
In a world without place,
and a child without a face.

Red

Red, an imaginary and forcible figure looking in upon herself,
abrupt and full of self-esteem she marches her way through deliberately made paths,
always heading forward, unconcerned with looking behind.
A straight back, square shoulders, eyes piercing every living thing,
neatly close cut hair, a solemn grimace look for all to see and read carefully.
No one stopping to argue with her or moving in and blocking her way,
she is a straight forward thinker with dark, neat garments,
yielding a sharpened blade at one side for all to gaze upon.
A blunt and defiant mind though not a foolish one,
long and powerful strides gripping the crumpled earth steadily,
seeking no companions or strangers to her call.
A gruff, sharp voice capable of shattering the silent air around her,
a very outgoing single minded person with no air of joy to be found,
only the cataclysm triumph of Red.

Chantelle Lowe

Relax

When I was your age,
I used to sit down on the grass,
and look out on the fields.

Resistance

Time is spoken without resistance,
a lie unsaid,
somewhere off into the distance,
something undid.
Hatred spilled, flowing like a torrent,
cascading in all forms.
It met others it should not have,
anger, and hideous in tone,
it was not meant to be.
Though it escaped to lie,
and falsely blame.
Misunderstanding, lying, whatever,
should not have been said,
but that it was,
and worse, that is what was meant.
It meant to lie, it meant to accuse,
it meant to hold out blame,

Chantelle Lowe

that is where I draw the line,
and will never be the same.
For where I found what truly was,
hideous, cruel and meant,
something which I did not want,
something which was only made of hate.
It laid out its cunning plan in all its finery,
that is where I knew I had to draw the line,
for this was something so hideous, not mine.

Chantelle Lowe

Retrospect

Placement and replacement in a whole.
Replacing the landscape which was most foreign.
Taking away this strange and derelict formation,
which took place in a most hostile environment.

Rise and soar

Place your hand in mine and see me for who I am,
unfold all the boundaries and make them visible.
Give me the strength to see myself out of this sham,
take away the obstructions which make me feeble.

Let me rise and soar to a higher state of mind,
from the restrictions given out by society.
Let me break free from the human chains that bind,
imagination to the state of misery.

Give me the power of existence to succeed,
and overcome the forces that bring destruction.
Give me the courage to go forward and lead,
in a world full of hurt and discrimination.

Let me find the way that paints the future,
of an extraordinary and wonderful picture.

Chantelle Lowe

Rivalry

Sabotaging the world to decay.
Congratulating others,
preparing to go beyond,
being out of touch.
Clambering into a world of the unknown.
Destroying atmospheres,
destroying minds.
Creating a downward turn,
into rivalry and frustration,
killing the minds and souls of others.

Chantelle Lowe

River running

River running, seething, thriving,
diving, splashing, culminating together.
River running, deep, narrow, windy,
rushing, thrashing, crashing.
River running, caressing the thoughts of the mind.
River diving, hovering against confinement,
concealing.
The jump, the fall,
the plunge into the liquid earth.
River running, do I see you?
River running, I can hear you.
River running over the edges of time and space.
River running over mind and soul.
River running over what is whole.

Rivulets

Splashing down the hill side,
caressing every step,
rocking all the stones wide,
with its vigorous hope.
Crashing down all the way,
to break down on the bay.
Though it does not always,
meet with the ocean's face,
some different paths take gaze,
on tracks without a trace.
Some lead to mountain floor,
while others lead to more.
Gaping, gazing around,
to make a path flatter,
where steps have been and found,
places new to splatter.
In hidden places made,

Chantelle Lowe

where no one comes to wade.
There it comes, splashing in,
where none do come or go.
Though some do peer within,
the current there to know,
a life lying under,
the stream's roaring thunder.

Say it soon

Say a little tune,
say it loud, say it soon.
Say it for me,
in the way that we see.
A divergence of the soul,
of what we thought whole.
Creating a new night,
in the dim of the light.
Where hope follows,
and faith goes.
Into the unseen world,
everything is hurled.
Taking in its place,
the unseen and unknown face.
Which rips at the fabric within,
the great and holy pin,
which appears as it is not.

Chantelle Lowe

The lying and hurtful blot
calling forth insanity,
when it should just let people be.

Search of relief

The ever branching soul turns calmly,
as it decides where to go.
Through forests of the night it hinders,
not seeing the ground below.

There is a voice to this traumatised soul,
it breathes moisture into the cold.
Sharpness tingles the skin through the wind,
leaving it feeling bold.

It comes here in search of relief,
from the memories.
Its torn and tattered life lies down,
in the midst of trees.

The comforting place it calls home,
away from the prying eye.

Shall fall

Time is eternity,
eternity is the rolling wheel.
Does it pull you under?
Does it hear you scream?
Time creates what cannot be foreseen,
what cannot be destroyed.
Time creates what is,
and cannot be undone.
To hold the knife of decision,
is a powerful thought.
To seize it, and use it,
is to create a will so strong.
The aftermath, concentrated in ripples,
will rip the fine web,
and shall fall.
Shall fall,
the knowledge of what has been done,

Chantelle Lowe

the knowledge to penetrate,
and perceive.
Shall fall,
destiny into another hand.
And thus sustain creation,
and recreation.

Chantelle Lowe

Shimmering secret

In the stagnant water,
is a well kept secret,
shimmering in the dullness.

Chantelle Lowe

Silence followed

So deep and yet so far,
as the avalanche pulled away,
into the dimness of all sight.
When the hand it did reach out,
I was appalled by the count, so many.
As if it were the right,
but no one chose to save the many,
as fire burned in the night,
I held the song of many, so loved, so near.
It chose me from the edges,
as the hurtling tide drew near,
it wasn't their fault I saw,
it wasn't their fault at all.
As they came in their numbers, I told,
in the silence followed, I stopped them all,
then I turned into the night so cold.
In the shock they were left to stand,

Chantelle Lowe

I merged myself to the background,
it took time for their own to stand,
as I walked in the shade, not found.

Chantelle Lowe

Soft black

In the dark of night,
I see the light,
of far above,
within the trees.
It touches down on all.

Chantelle Lowe

Soft blue

Clear and brittle,
with the frequency of generations intertwined.
Smooth with a piercing and thorough stare,
violent at any provocation.
Yet it is almost impossible to disturb it,
it peers through all.

Soft green

Fearful, peaceful,
calm and array,
cowardice yet bold,
in its own little way.
Stepping for the behind,
the wise,
as only the courageous will fall.

Chantelle Lowe

Soft purple

Mysterious and motivated,
colourful yet elegant,
infectious to all,
it appeals to none.

Chantelle Lowe

Soft red

Warm with subtlety,
it sweeps like a rage infecting all,
taking the uttermost courage to break free.
For it soaks in deep,
and no memory can get rid of it.

Chantelle Lowe

Soft wind

The fog came rolling over the hill,
but how was I to know,
and how was I to forget.
The damp fresh forest smell,
swirling over the soft wind.

Chantelle Lowe

Soft yellow

Fake and faltering,
in its content.
It seems to cover all,
spring has brought them thus,
I see.

Solitary being

In the room of the solitary being,
where fragments grow,
from eternal thoughts seeping forward,
into question.
I hear my calling,
to be answered.
Where the thoughts rage through my head,
and the passing of time sweeps them away,
into the darkness.
Where out of the old,
new things grow,
and come to pass, fleeting away,
with what has born them, so strong.
Into the dying ashes,
to be forgotten,
yet still remembered.
Nonetheless,

Chantelle Lowe

no one hears,
what has been done,
in lying and deceit.
To penetrate,
no questions asked,
to what has made the whole.
No calm, no quiet,
where flooding waters rage.
Silently, yet ever so strong,
when no voice can be cried out.
For the eternal suffering is too great,
for the mind's interpretation,
and no one can find what has been lost.
When nothing has been gained to lose,
in this eternal suffering of all that has been.

Still searching

Culminating ideas from the whole,
not wanting to break up the soul.
I took it with me to see it again,
though I know it not, as I knew it then.
An image creased out on an aged old page,
showing the journey and views of advantage.
I wanted something to show, I wanted something to glow,
yet I am still searching, still yearning.
A special place lifted up,
seeing the path below,
seeing everything,
searching amidst the worldly positions,
to find obscurity.

Strength

Let all the wind blow east,
into the falling sun.
Then in the fading light,
what is right will be done.

Call forth toward the open spirit,
the one which has protected thee.
Bring it forth with open arm,
for all the world to see.

Take this as a gift of love,
use it wisely on the ground.
Where turmoil seeps through,
and struggle is all around.

Give with all the power and might,
to create a change and fight.

Strength in voices

I wait and I hear the strength in others voices,
carrying me away into other places.
Calmly listening to the sounds of their choices,
it was pleasing to see the interested faces.

I do not know if I said it right,
in fact I am not sure at all.
The adrenaline has left that held me tight,
when I stood up and answered the call.

Sun shines warmly on my pen through the window,
smiling, praising me as if to know.

Chantelle Lowe

Substance

Love is the being which creates the soul.
A substance which is greatly forgotten
amidst a turbulent world,
with its vision of violence,
perpetrating the souls of youths.

Table of time

I sit here at the table of time, and I sit alone.
I sit here as the years go by, and all I have is my own.
I sit here with the grace not bestowed on me, but the grace that had to be.
It flowed from no ones hand but mine, for the grace no one gave entwined.
The soul perplexed for what was brought, and all in time it came to nought.
I rise with the knowledge that carries in my soul,
a picture of turmoil caught within the whole.
For what was and could not be was the source of so much pain,
yet the way before had nothing left to gain.
As the door closed and I took from it the one regret,
that in this time I shall not forget.
Time has sealed its fate for the fallen, taking with it the memories stolen.
Perhaps not for me it cries in the shadows that rage,
for I have no more to give upon this stage.

Tactics

Tactics of war, tactics of hate,
emotional blackmail,
emotional disgrace.
Negative input degenerating the soul,
feeding to worthlessness.
Igniting pessimism from within.
Angry negative overtones,
arrayed with subtle put downs,
a creative which emulates hate.
Despising the opening of the world,
and together with all this hate,
it reaches for the souls of many,
lashing out its pain,
and hateful blame.

Chantelle Lowe

Take me away

Take me away,
take me away,
to a better place,
the final grace,
pure anticipation,
waiting for the mention,
of the sterile game,
which makes all the same.
Take me away,
to a better place,
take me away,
to the final grace.
I left without a care,
if you were there,
when the reason was clear,
I left you to sear.
Take me away,

Chantelle Lowe

all I wanted to say,
was lost in your face,
from that other place.
Take me away,
to the final grace.

Take no ones hand

Darkness fills the night,
the illumination fills my soul.
Here I have been,
as many have before.
I take no ones hand,
as I grasp into the unseen.
Bellowing, flowing into the atmosphere,
here is where I see,
into the dark crevices that make up
the unknown.
I am not here as someone else,
I am here as what makes me who I am.

Take the past away

Dark is the day I see,
which I do not understand.
It is all I know of the past,
it is all I used to have.
Now that I have come from that,
I do not accept it into my life.
Taking my past away,
Is too difficult,
so instead I live on,
leaving it out of my current life.

Taking grasp

Trouble, stability.
Carrying forth in old memories.
Taking a grasp on the present.
Reaching out to whatever was taken.
It placed a hold on reality,
touching the souls around it.
It had nothing good to give,
only anger, hatred and pain.

Talking

I am calling out,
I hear voices.
To my dismay, I do not know what they say.
I just hear sounds, and I know they are talking.
Voices, sounds, reverberation,
of sound into the void.
Can I call it my own, when it is not?
Characters which call out to me,
using my thoughts.
Telling me things,
voicing out load what I want to be.

Taunting

The world of understanding is not the one I know.
It comes and goes, fleeting past,
occupying my mind.
Interpreting my thoughts, gripping at my mind,
taunting me from all around.

The chase

Too easy to please,
too quick to define,
was she to those who all knew.
Yet flaunting her ways,
did nothing to gaze,
for her tricks were all shallow and cruel.
For note within time,
she played five or nine,
all searching for something more deep.
But, she with her fine airs and grace,
delighted in having the race,
to see which one spent more,
every time.

Chantelle Lowe

The forgotten land

Filling in time,
of the forgotten land,
where centuries past,
comes forth their hand.

Chantelle Lowe

The humble architect

The humble architect is a creature I know not which,
it exists in the parallels of time.
A creature born of an unusual nature,
possessing strength and determination in essence.
Calling on the pasts of many,
to divulge their ultimate meanings.

The intrepid walk to eternity

Besieged by the one thing I love yet I know I cannot stay,
as it wraps around my mortal coil and plays so placidly.
For on the shore's great timeless depth another chance does sway,
glimmering in the distant waves crashing down into the sea.

No lover to hold me back and no one to take me forward,
for all the ill that time laps before my door I cannot stay.
I wish I could in heart but the turmoil holds me in retreat,
what say you if we walk along the shores upon this day?

As I turn the other way my mind starts to crumble in fear,
it etches at my soul's desire and taunts the ones I love.
I feel my sorrow grow for I know not how long I am here,
I wonder if it is meant to be as I face the storm above.

For fleeting past calls misery like an awkward game of chance,
and no lover's hand can still my heart in the fading hour's rant.

Chantelle Lowe

If not long I was meant to be then let known for just a glance,
the day that remembers the air of a mother's loving chant.

As voices raised in a vibrant cheer call from near then pass,
in a time not so long ago in the filter of one's eye.
'Tis not what I have reckoned as I peer at an empty glass,
the time taken then lost again in a deep resounding sigh.

For hope's past and a long road held on a dusty mantle,
my wavering hand brushes past in the calm cool breeze.
For no mortal eye can fathom the darkness that I grapple,
yet I ponder the time I have in a peaceful resting ease.

One step before another in the distant memory,
of a life half lived fading with the crimson coloured sky.
For I shall pass the time with an air filled grace of love and be,
searching deep for the kindest stare and a cheery hopeful eye.

In the darkest hour of life on the edge of mortality,
I will reach above the horizon's gaze and hope there will be.

Chantelle Lowe

The sea of reason

When the sea comes it will be shallow with reason,
and I will take it in my arms and cuddle it,
with the deepest of meaning and the softest kindness,
I will wade into it and let it smother me.

Chantelle Lowe

The sea turns

When the sea turns green my heart will return in immortal sadness,
to conquer my fears eternally in the eclipse of the world to be.
I shall set fire to my soul to burn away the hatred of others,
and then shall I return to my rightful place deep inside of me.

Chantelle Lowe

The soldier of dusk

In the light of the Monday Moon,
I sailed across the Seventh Star,
to find the Tenth Tower,
upon the ledge of the Ruined River,
to seek a break in the Dry Dusk.

To grasp the shadow of the Melting Monument,
on the dark side of the Solid Stone,
to leak across the Tanned Terrain,
to crumble and melt into my Revered Reunion,
then I shall seek the peace of the Destined Death.

Chantelle Lowe

The timid

Like disciples of the night I see them fly,
their elegant gowns touch the ground they walk on,
their graciousness shows their simultaneous movement as gentle.
The whisper of their padded feet and waving cloaks tells me they are near,
their timidness shows in their hooded faces.

The way it had to be

For what it is worth,
do I not see too,
what has been done on this earth,
without the help of you?

I do not see a day gone by,
when I do not think,
of the reason why,
you had to sink.

But I knew far too well,
it had just begun,
this is when I had to tell,
of all that had been done.

Do not blame the people you hurt,
do not put blame on me,

Chantelle Lowe

when you treated us like dirt,
this was the way it had to be.

Chantelle Lowe

Thinking about Burnie

The world revolves around a single thought, or does it?
Underneath the undercurrents of its belly lies the turmoil of its roaring power,
lapping up against the wind swept shore in a salty fit.
I came and stood at the bottom of the rain's rolling tower,
which swept through my fingers and down the pores of my face.
I wanted to hide and run from its path, but there was nowhere it did not reach.
It touched the ends of all my thoughts gliding through the place,
and played at the tips of my toes gripping into the beach.
The wind's roar broken with the activity by my right,
the crates all gathered on the asphalt platform gathering rust,
and the little feet playing on the grass in the light,
as the seagulls fly through the wind and dust.
Here I stand with the cold tickling my pores,
and no amount of energy can compel me away.
For where the city meets the plain of the ravaged shores,

Chantelle Lowe

the feel of the sea calms me in its own special way.

Travelling in from the shores soft sand and up the windy road,
fleeing past cottage houses and busy streets filled with colour,
I come to rest in the most serene beauty and feel my thoughts unload.
For here the water rushes past and into the bottom to stir,
with its roar gliding through the trees and over the rocks below,
taking my dreams further a field out to the seabed's floor.
Far have I come to wonder where the future will go,
tracing the steps of other people gone before.
A little while seems a lifetime as the water swirls around,
not wanting to stay still or stop for anyone.
As it continues its way and covers ground,
somewhere in the middle of this it sees what has begun.
A thought washed away to the new frontier,
the steaming hub of life far below the graceful sight,
and in amidst all of this I stop and shed a tear,
for all my thoughts have led me now down to the township site.
Walking near the hard workers at the wharf and through the smiling faces,
I hear someone say hello and I know everything is going to be all right.
For as the steady stream goes on of people going through their paces,
the world goes on as one thought takes flight.

Chantelle Lowe

Through the gloom

Ambiguities in necessities,
accomplishments made and lost,
yet the triumph is always the same.
I meet the conclusion face on,
opposing opposition,
to find my way through the gloom.
It is an interesting journey,
I take through the pages of time.
Not appealing to anyone,
is the wrath I left behind.
Though it was not confronted,
it was left behind.
Away from imagination,
away from the mind's eye,
away from determination.

Time eternal

In the darkness before the dawn I cry like no other,
for a tale long lost in the ever changing breeze.
For a time placed indistinguishably then left to smother,
over the unforeseen with a fine intrepid ease.

If not for me then not for any other shall it course,
into the undeniable ambiguity of the greatest peril.
For I have held witness to the darkest night in pause,
as the trembling quivers down the seeds that tell.

In a glowing flame spread throughout belying reason,
the sadness stirs slowly creeping into the creases.
As my mind wavers in its bleakest hour of the season,
and all hope vanquishes from the hand as time ceases.

In the darkest hour before the dawn I gain my final strength,
not knowing the time eternal or its full length.

Chantelle Lowe

Time to unwind

Down, down with the soul I dreaded so much,
an apathy which haunts still in the morning light.
No such luck avails me now,
for all I thought has come to pass.
It is a long and lonely journey which calls me now,
deep from the hollows that have yet to unwind.
All I want is myself and a little time,
yet this seems far from the truth.
I walk as I have many times before,
and every time the journey seems the same.
Finding my own way in a great deal of disarray,
it is not the easy way to find oneself.
All I wanted was a bit of time,
yet I do not think I have found it.

Chantelle Lowe

To be confident

Waiting for the final moment to arrive,
waiting hurriedly,
excited and scared all at the same time.
I do not know what to expect,
I have to be confident,
and extremely self determined,
especially to get this far.

Chantelle Lowe

To be strong

I know I am different
when I see myself
for who I am,
I know I am someone else
and this is me.
My identity comes from many places
deep with in my life.
Some of them I hate,
and some I cherish.
Life is never what it seems,
and it comes back to haunt me.
When I have come such a long way,
I do not want to be a part
of my ugly past.
So I left it out of my life,
and I know I have to be strong.
All I want more than anything else

Chantelle Lowe

is to be me.

To crush myself

Did I take a sip of your wine?
Did I grasp what you wanted?
Is it the idea that compels you?
That I know too much.
Take my hand and you would see eternity,
but would it scare you?
Like so many others.
Are you too late to see me go?
For when I leave it is forever.
Did you ever know what I was?
When you bent me to your creation,
did you ever know what you destroyed?
Now it is gone forever,
because I will not see you again.
You may have destroyed a part of me,
but I will not ever destroy,
what I have left.

Chantelle Lowe

To crush myself,
is a worse crime than what you have done.

To end the pain

Is it so hard,
to determine reality,
when there is none?
I see you,
in oblivion.
Do you need,
the distraction of life,
to know,
evil is what you make it to be?
But no one knows for sure,
am I really here, any more?
To create a darkness so deep,
in eternity,
is to weep a million deaths.
All names to be withered away,
with the morning sun,
of destiny.

Chantelle Lowe

Do you hear them calling,
out,
reaching out?
I see them,
their undying hand,
gives way to misery,
and I sear their pain.

Chantelle Lowe

To flee

I did not see the wall of stone,
which held me tight.
Though I knew I had to flee,
with all my might,
no person came to guide my way.

Chantelle Lowe

To know who I am

Two children playing a game of catch,
two wounds to lay to heal.
Three side ways glances,
three times to know,
the threat which has come is real.
Four marks for the score,
four ways to the door,
Five ways of seeing through.
five things which count,
when the way is not seen as before.
Six things which matter,
six ways of flight.
Seven who know,
seven to hold me tight,
in the glimpse of all that is not right.
Eight to mend the way ahead,
eight to make it steady.

Chantelle Lowe

Nine to see the going rough,
nine to see me back,
where I know I will be ready.
Ten to call out to where I am,
ten to place a caring hand.
One to know where I will be,
one to know who I am,
when there is no one here left to stand.

Chantelle Lowe

Traces left behind

And in the dark, the forest bites,
I hear your calling,
like the stream of an echoed time,
slipping steadily away from my fingers,
and onto the crumbled ground below.
I picked up a leaf, one day,
it was dying.
I could see the decay,
as I crumpled it in my fist.
The breeze came,
and took what was left away.
But in my hand,
I could still feel its fragile surface,
and the taint of the life it once had,
now gone.
Gone from this world, gone from these stars,
but not from my mind.

Chantelle Lowe

As I closed my eyes, in reflection of myself,
I could see the leaf as I was,
as it fell under the strains I had wrought.
I looked closely at my own palm,
and saw only the lifelessness,
of what the leaf had left behind.

Chantelle Lowe

Transgression

Practising illuminating transgression
of the soul,
collaborating with the infinity
of a whole.
Replacing the ambiguities
of the mind,
destroying the fabric
of a kind.

Trembling

Trembling down my spine,
turning me down the pages of the road,
which guides me into the unknown.
Did you see which way I went?
For I know not the extent of the situation.
Closing along the fine line of thread,
which covers my soul from the top of the earth to the top of my head.
Taking away the ground beneath and the translation of what was read.
How can it be that the truth is marred with such resistance,
that it calls out not knowing,
which way it went.
Can I find you?
Did I see which way you went?
Do not call me as a last resort,
for I am none.
The tranquillity leaves me far behind,
and with it went my colourful state of mind.

Turmoil

Most people do not see,
the way all things can be.
With every hour that sees the sky,
and all the turmoil lost nearby.
Why can't I seek what I have heard,
when no one sees the written word?
But all is not lost from what was done,
for no one could see the setting sun,
for which is sheltered in the palm of my hand,
to throw and shake the embodied land.
In its hatred of the unseen eternity,
plummeting forth on all to see.

Chantelle Lowe

Undetermined path

Intrepid is the soul that follows,
the undetermined path.
A creation of the whereabouts,
an indescribable task.
Unfortunately as the tide flows in,
matters became exceedingly clear.
A homage to the other world,
a desire that draws them there.

Chantelle Lowe

Ultimate goal

And I pick myself up, and I pick myself up.
And I take it to its highest height.
I take it away from the world's dim light.
The grey that covers all our thoughts,
the depression in the hole.
I have to pick myself up out of this,
to accomplish the ultimate goal.

Vanish

The fire burns bright on the souls of the many,
dimly shadowing the past with colours untold,
I know not these people, as once I thought I did,
and the world it changes showing these souls differently.
I cry over their loss, I cry for knowing they had been better,
I mourn their change for the worse,
I mourn as they willingly turn down the path.
Brazenly going into a cold and silent light,
silhouetting their forms as they turn their backs.
Nothing I can say will make them stay,
as they turn they smile with triumph,
ignorant on the things they will be missing.
Things they valued as precious,
and I see them turn away and vanish.
They change, and I do not know if I am seeing the real them.

Virus

Killer, killer.
Do I see you,
inside of me?
Will you wipe away the tears of anguish
that accumulate in my soul?
Will you take me with you
when everything is made whole?
Killer, killer.
Do you see me,
as I see you?

Waiting for friends

My fingers tingled to my bones,
the streaks of changing shapes,
moved across the surface.
I played for a time,
and I lulled to myself.
The wet stormy night trickled down,
and I wondered how I was going to get back.
I was amidst a sea of people doing the same,
waiting,
as I waited I knew it was for something important,
friends.

Washed away

Time carries past no fear,
with it the darker day,
renews the place so near,
with all the reasons washed away.

Place it by your side and see,
if all the memories travel past.
In a way to form what should not be,
in the shape of the shadow cast.

Will you place it in my hand,
the treasures worth more than gold?
Let it grow into the land,
until I am too old.

Then with all the memories that will crease,
I and time will come to cease.

Chantelle Lowe

Was it important?

Where I was,
where I came from.
Where did I go?
What did I do?
But was it important?
Had it anything to do with me?
Was I supposed to listen?
I don't think so,
though I can't be sure.

Chantelle Lowe

Waves folding

In the waves which folded, lapping over the last,
a hand stirred the fringes of its foamy lace.
It beckoned to the onlooker as the water fell past,
and flowed forwards, roaring, gaining strength, then losing pace.
It was beautiful yet timid as it broke through the surface,
flinging itself skywards with its momentum,
in its eyes it smiled.

Chantelle Lowe

Way ahead

No life brightens more, than the life you have and lead,
which calls to you and leads you away.
Not knowing where to guide you,
when the way ahead remains unclear.

Chantelle Lowe

What could be

Can I see the eternal mind,
reaching forth,
into form and grace.
No place have I found,
where time stands still,
for peace and the ending
of what has been.
For what could be,
is not.

What holds me

No time, no place,
to land my feet,
I am no prisoner here.
What holds me,
and sustains my life,
is the essence of all eternity.
Give me your hand,
dispel all the myths,
which have been given,
and take the path which belongs.
Am I gone,
to the time I have created?
Where no hope remains,
where there is no reason.

Chantelle Lowe

What I have become

One day I looked down onto the earth,
to see where I may fit in.
It spoke to me from the pages of old,
calling me away from this life,
and into another.
It colours my soul,
I drape around me what I have become,
stepping out further into this unknown path,
do I know myself?
I know what I am not,
yet so many people see me as such,
because they are unable to see,
what I have become,
and what was meant to be.

Chantelle Lowe

When my path was for one

In the path of lighted shadows do I hear it call untoward,
how do I know this, when all appears to be lost?
The stranger seeks unusual company as it appears again, unknowing,
yet do I need its company where I sit and stand?
For all alone am I, in this world I traverse,
and not one shall see it different as the rains steadily pass.
To sit, I did not know myself, yet some may say otherwise,
in the reaches of the whole.
Nothing compares as it once did, when my path was all for one,
and no one knew me otherwise, in the quiet little place.

Chantelle Lowe

When no one calls

I see a clear blue sky,
landing on the horizon.
What do I see,
when all is gone forever?
Clearly I know nothing,
when everybody else does not know.
What can the answer be,
when I am lost?
Do I hear the caller,
in a time long gone?
Do I rise to the shadow,
when no one calls?
Is this what we all came for,
when there was no more?
I see what is done,
to replace the imaginable.
This is sin,

Chantelle Lowe

to create something foreseen,
when all is not lost.
Do I hope to disappear,
when time itself has fled?
This is a reason,
I cannot hear.
When everybody else sees,
what is done,
and I cannot.
For it is not the piece I want,
from a whole.
Do I not see the faces,
feel the fear,
when there is nothing left,
to reason with,
but our own despair?
I hear no other voice,
but it is not I it will take,
off into the uncaring.
For I have seen what has been wrought,
with dislike and temptation,
the ebbing of the fear,
this thing I will not tolerate.
Do I not feel its senses,

Chantelle Lowe

corroding with time.
I have not made it here,
to be destroyed again.
I will see a new way,
with those, I care for.

When the wind blows

As mist rolled out in finer spray,
to play a part in cold array.
It circled higher in cold night air,
as figure seen made a dare.

No friend or foe stood in place,
to watch the dangerously fatal race.
As voice of mine did roll and spin,
creature upon thy cheek did grin.

Merciless it echoed sound,
with colder tentacles than were found,
on one and whom I laid to catch,
for mighty was he, an equal match.

As sweat of mine turned to ice,
cold fragment on my skin did slice.

Chantelle Lowe

On face and throat as time grew near,
   upon this moment I did hear.

Through ice shallow and broken wind,
   heartbeats not my own were pinned.
   In close of range as ice drew thick,
on stilled air where no sound did pick.

As my hand held tight around its throat,
   the frozen ice did vanish in one note.
   Mist fell away to let warmth shine,
   and stray cat in my arms was mine.

When rain turns to thunder

I can hear the raindrops turning into thunder,
it is my destiny screaming through my age,
I can feel its soul hiding behind my eyes,
it is whispering to my unconscious self,
it is breaking through.

Chantelle Lowe

Within a place

Colours of strange design,
spread across the landscape,
shaping and moulding our eyes.
Placing what is underneath on display,
creating a place, which is a place
within one.
Making the difference between harsh and comfortable,
bringing forth the feeling from submergence.
Creating a shape unique to another,
which sits within its shell.
Embracing the landscape further to encompass,
the continuation of a whole.

Chantelle Lowe

World apart

When I go 'round,
I find a place,
no one can trace,
what I have found.

Then I go back,
and see the earth,
for all it's worth,
far down the track.

But here I see,
my own mind framed,
on what it aimed,
for all to be.

A world apart,
placed at the start.

Would it matter?

To be designed in a way which matters,
recognising attribution which gives way.
When finally we perceive what is,
although into what I do not know.
Come forth and hear, though not what you thought,
it is so strange, that way.
But what if, or not,
killing time as it were, with everything it has.
Come forth I have, through faith and glory,
concealing misery and pain from memories,
does it matter when it is now?
Would it ever matter in the way that I see it?
This is an open mind, crushed by harshness,
and even though I do not see further.
I hope that it will be the case,
that I ride through this disaster,
but now I am sure that this has taken effect.

Chantelle Lowe

Though I wanted it not to be so.

Yellow

Yellow sits by herself, musing with a leaf between her fingers,
rushing through the long grass, peering up to the sky.
Laughing aloud, calling to the flocks of many birds,
dancing in the breeze, with a thin, light coloured wavy dress.
Pattering her small feet against the soft springy grass,
long wavy light coloured hair flowing free.
Arms raised to the clouds, legs skipping along with ease,
sparkly, dancing eyes viewing the immense colours everywhere.
On the ground, in the trees, on the birds, in the sky, on the lake,
warming the heart of yellow.

www.ingramcontent.com/pod-product-compliance
Lightning Source LLC
Chambersburg PA
CBHW060526010526
44107CB00059B/2613